Startled by Faith

new poetry in traditional forms

FEATURING

J.S. Absher

edited by Laura Vosika

Gabriel's Horn Publishing

Copyright 2025 by Laura Vosika and Gabriel's Horn Press

All rights reserved. No portion of this book may be reproduced, stored in any retrieval system, or transmitted in any form or by any means electronic, mechanical, photocopy, recording, scanning, or other except for brief quotations in reviews or articles, without the prior written permission of the author and publisher.

Cover Design: Laura Vosika

Contact gabrielshornpress@gmail.com

Published in the United States by Gabriel's Horn Press

First printing 2025 in the United States

For sales, visit www.gabrielshornpress.com

PRINT ISBN: 979-8-88846-013-9

Other Books by Gabriel's Horn

The Blue Bells Chronicles: a tale of time travel….
- *Blue Bells of Scotland*
- *The Minstrel Boy*
- *The Water is Wide*
- *Westering Home*
- *The Battle is O'er*

Food and Feast in the World of the Blue Bells Chronicles: a gastronomic historic poetic musical romp in thyme

Shawn Brink: *The Space Between* trilogy

My Gypsy War Diary

Gabriel's Horn Poetry Anthologies, collator/editor
- Startled by JOY: 2019
- Startled by NATURE: 2020
- Startled by LOVE: 2021
- Startled by HUMOR: 2022
- Startled by MUSIC 2023

Laurie Kehoe: *Dreams of Dragons*

Ilona Miler: *A Woman of Many Names*

Dan Blum: *The Feet Say Run*

Lilly Gelle: *Gypsy Heart*

Dr. Chris R. Powell: *The Path that Shines: a story of life, love, and loss*

Rebecca May Hope *Shattered Faith*

Silken Strands

Destination Harmony

…and many more

STARTLED
BY
FAITH

featuring

J.S. ABSHER

STARTLED BY FAITH

Creator and Creation	1
Praise and Thanks	17
Prayer	31
Daily Life	39
Trust in Hard Times	45
Faith and Doubt	57
Redemption	65
From the Bible	83
Death & the Afterlife	99
Poetry Forms	107
Poet Bios	111
Featured Poet	112
All Poets	113

Creator & Creation

First, there was God
Then there was light
Then day and night
Animals on land, fish in the sea
Then He made man—you and me

Earthworm Lore

In the lore of the nightcrawler and red wriggler,
it's said that, when Jesus knelt and wrote in the dust,
their progenitors saw it from below
(saw it, though they had no eyes!)—
two vertical lines for the tree of life, and two
along the bottom for the river of life.`
As He wrote, they saw those lines also engraved
on the wide palm of His hand, framing the names
He'd made and blessed, billions of us, written
in vanishingly small
nanoscale, miraculously legible
letters. And some say, on a golden wall
of the Holy of Holies in heaven are two
upright lines, the trees of wisdom and life;
two horizontal, for the waters we drink
from once and never again thirst;
and squiggly lines for the Annelida
underfoot: these least that shall be first.

Startled by FAITH

And they say Jesus saw the little worms
and promised: You will enrich the soil of Zion
and restore the loam of Eden. When My hands
that rolled you from clay and mud
are pierced, you will see the fount of red
composting death with vivifying blood.

— J.S. Absher

Form: The first 3 and last 2 lines of each stanza are in loose iambic pentameter; the fourth line is in tetrameter or trimeter and rhymes with the last line.

Publication credits:
Mormon Lit Blitz, Fall 2023;
Amethyst Review, August 2023

Science Class

When it rained, not water droplets, condensation,
but God eating tomatoes, Big Boys, Super Sweets,
dripping juice, bending over the nations,
noshing and biting with marble white teeth.
When lightning flashed, not thermal emissions,
but God snapping photos if you please,
picture day, the Cherubim and Seraphim,
selfies by the pearly gates, "Say cheese!"
When thunder boomed, not gas expanding,
but angels bowling in a tournament,
a thunderclap, God's grandstanding,
perpetual strikes, applause in the firmament.
When fireflies flashed, not bio-phosphorescence,
but tiny lanterns, messengers from above,
Tinkerbells, not light in tumescence,
luminous visitors like stars, like love.

When there's death, not irreversible cessation
of circulation, respiration, brain function,
but a heavenly ancestral jubilation,
another sort of life, assumption.

— Donna Isaac
Rhyming quatrains

Stump

Upon the way I came
The world alight with only trees
The deer and me, the birds, the breeze
Expecting it should so remain
      As solitary as when I passed

And so it did, and yet, at last
I came upon a jumbled heap of wood
Piled high above my head it stood
And to one side, some ten feet wide,
Logs and cords all freshly cut

Neither the deer nor birds nor trees
Had left such handiwork as these
No man appeared, nor crossed this land
Yet surely this was done by conscious hand

And so upon a stump I sit
And on another rest my feet
As if made for me—footrest and chair
Could any accident be so neat?
No. I'm not alone, another has passed there
He chooses to hide, perhaps he watches from the wood
And smiles as I sit on the stump he crafted for me with care

— Angela Rose
Rhyming verse

Villanelle in Prayer

My sanctuary a cathedral of trees.
They stand on an undulating floor.
Into a holy canopy they squeeze.

Others gather to pray on knees,
but I have been here before.
My sanctuary a cathedral of trees.

No choir, no organ, no celestial fees,
a symphony of motion as in days of yore.
Into a holy canopy they squeeze.

Light drops through the colander like grated cheese.
Strands keep falling until they pour.
My sanctuary a cathedral of trees.

I look to the Heavens my heart to seize.
I'm deep in prayer, a standing encore.
Into a holy canopy they squeeze.

Lacy webs visible after fog flees.
Glistening landlord has spun a villa galore.
My sanctuary a cathedral of trees.
Into a holy canopy they squeeze.

— Evie Groch
Villanelle

Stalking the Deer

How softly did that deer appear
On yester-eve and then again today
Such that I thought it should always be here
Whenever I might come this way

So with camera here I come
To photograph his elegant grace
Instead I find myself quite alone
(Oh deer! He's broken our steady date!)
Just me and the breeze in this wooded place

I thought I'd capture him with ease
Just show up in our grove
It looks as thought I must work harder
      Seek him further

Startled by FAITH

Likewise, Jesus came to me
Once or twice at my slightest prayer
I quickly came to believe
That He would always be waiting there

But no! Like the deer, he's only lured me in
Started me along a path
Of craving another glimpse of Him

— J.A. Sellers
Quatrains

Where Did Yesterday Go?

Difficult to say where yesterday went
a simple question but hard to solve it
ordinary day appears a riddle
the rotation of earth may be a source
a cloud disappears with hardly a trace
a season proceeds in a stately pace
the beats of a heart reliably pace

afternoon shower descended and went
the vapor of an ocean is a source
the puddles on my driveway are a trace
the roots of the trees depend upon it
the beauty of the clouds is a riddle

poignancy of beauty is a riddle
the wrinkles of the skin come with a pace
memory of youth is a sticky trace
necessary to burst and grow from it
triumph and disappointment came and went
a blossom of consciousness is a source

evanescence of a bloom is a source
the arc of a lifetime is a riddle
a burdened person needs to accept it
quicksilver success so easily went
opportunity and loss have a pace
family embodies a mighty trace

intimacy propagates echoes trace
love and grief are inevitable source
intricate connections so quickly went
network of people establishes pace
undigested motive is a riddle
curiosity helps to distinguish it

leverage of urgency compels it
decades of circumstance clarify trace
diminished choices accumulate pace
the peace of forgiveness is a riddle
immeasurable dismay is a source
eventually anguish peaked and went

where yesterday went we do not know it
mind is a riddle that questions its source
the seams of earth are trace of a pace.

— Tekkan
Sestina

Sand

To see completely and to understand
the ocean flows without a memory
the rocks will dissolve into grains of sand

granite mountains dominate the land
they brave the sky without anxiety
to see completely and to understand

there is a bloom of life within grasslands
the earth delights in wild variety
the rocks will dissolve into grains of sand

only for a while do the mountains stand
mountains crumble without impiety
to see completely and to understand

the beginning and ending are not planned
humans enjoy a weird society
the rocks will dissolve into grains of sand

nature transforms with invisible hands
seasons evolve with odd propriety
to see completely and to understand
the rocks will dissolve into grains of sand.

— Tekkan
Villanelle

Faithful bumblebee

Faithful bumble bee
Science says he cannot fly
He believes he can.

— Jerri Hardesty
Haiku

Praise & Thanks

When Israel marched by night or day
The tribe of Judah led the way
Judah's name means PRAISE
Let us lead with praise all our days

Abecedarian Alleluia

And when the song which had long lain silent
began to vibrate with a renewed insistent
call for peace through valleys and hills and forests in
distant lands, in cities and villages, the homed and homeless all heard
echos reverberate in every dialect of every
foreign tongue - a modern tower of Babel - and people, once defeated
grew restless as awakened from a deep slumber, as
hope sprouted like the first blooms after winter snows
inside desolate and aching hearts —
jostling into renewed life reaching out with
kindness and generosity, expressing freshly found
love for the differently designed and
manifestations and infiltrations of
new beings, new ways of being,
opening the eyes of the myopic to the
possibility for beauty beyond oneself as if
quarried from endless
rainbows, and mined from earth's bounty - no
species more valued or esteemed
than any other, finally together
united in the desire for belonging —

variegated voices and presentations
with a chorus of inclusion rising and reaching those once
xed out or discarded,
you and I and all creation
zigzagging throughout the earth, living the Alleluia.

— deb y. felio
Abecederian poem

An Ode to Faith

Part I: The Golden Foundation

In the heart of the tempest, where the wind doth roar,
A golden beacon stands, steadfast evermore.
Its luster, a testament to the faith that we hold,
A treasure more precious than any gold.

The gilded rays of dawn break through the night,
Illuminating paths with their warm, golden light.
Like a bird in flight, our spirits take wing,
Carried aloft by faith's eternal spring.

Part II: The Avian Anthem

Upon the zephyr's breath, the birds do sing,
Their melodies a hymn to the divine.
With feathers agleam like threads of pure gold,
They soar above, their stories untold.

The rushing wind whispers secrets old,
Of courage and hope, and hearts so bold.
In its embrace, we find our release,
Faith's gentle touch, our souls' sweet peace.

So let us cherish this sacred trust,
In faith's embrace, we find our rest.
For like the birds and gold that gleam,
Our faith is a dream that flows like a stream.

— C.R. Powell
Ballad

Incarnation

Like Job, I had no umpire
To reconcile me to God.
Nor snow, nor lye, nor work of mine
Could cleanse my hands from blood.
But a baby born in Bethlehem
To be my mediator
Closed the rift. His unspeakable gift
Joined me to my Creator.

I had no sufficient sacrifice
To make atonement for my sin,
No priest to heed my spirit's need
Who himself was pure within.
But a baby born in Bethlehem
Became my sympathetic priest.
His offering was everything;
The sacrifice has ceased.

Startled by FAITH

I had no one to imitate
In humility, faith, and love.
The godly walk was merely talk
Without power from above.
But a baby born in Bethlehem
Who died on Calvary
Stands by my side, my faithful guide,
To love and humility.

So what does incarnation mean?
This baby in a stall
Died for my sin to intervene,
To ransom from the Fall.
My Umpire and my great High Priest,
My example in peace and danger,
Came humbly dressed, an unwelcome guest,
As a babe in the Bethlehem manger.

— Rebecca May Hope
Ballad, iambic tetrameter with abcbdefe;
Internal rhymes on lines 3 and 7 of each stanza

Thanksgiving

Misery by the roadside sat,
Crying, "Unclean! Unclean!"
Whenever passerby approached
Or human face was seen.

Misery ripened to despair
At hearing, "No cure but death."
A dread disease, disfigurement,
And slow decay of health.

Despair encountered loneliness:
Without family or friend,
Long days were spent in idleness
Just waiting for the end.

Despair, misery, loneliness
Looked up with clouded eyes
To see the vacant valley where
The western vulture flies.

But look! Across the vale moves one
Whose face removes disaster.
Misery leaps now to his feet
And cries out, "Mercy, Master!"

The Master hears, the Master heals
At seeing a spark of faith.
Another falling soul is snatched
From off the brink of death.

The healed one turns. With all his breath
He glorifies the Lord.
Nine others with him, also healed,
The healer have ignored.

My case? 'Twas as—no, more—severe
As what the leper endured.
Alien from the Commonwealth,
Without hope, without God in the world.

Christ died for me. As an enemy
I had spilled the God-man's blood.
Yet He so loved, yes, He so gave
As no friend ever could.

And I? Should I not glorify
The One who cleansed my soul
And with His life's blood sacrifice
Made this leper whole?

— Rebecca May Hope
Ballad with alternating iambic tetrameter and iambic trimeter lines with abcb.

After Emmaus

"Seek not the living among the dead!"
Well had the tomb-guarding angel said.
"He is not here," for how could He be?
He is in Heaven; He pleads for me.

Did not our hearts burn within us then
As He unfolded what he had been
Doing and finishing from the start—
Laid it before us as if on a chart?

Only by shedding of blood, his own,
Could He ascend to His rightful throne,
Henceforth expecting His enemies
To be brought to Him upon their knees.

After He by Himself purged our sin,
He passed through the veil and entered in,
Delivered us who through fear of death
Were subject to bondage with every breath.

Vict'ry of victories when He died:
Death's fearful power was crucified.
Now we who live should live for Him
Who died to redeem us from bonds of sin.

Through suffering He learned obedience,
Against our accuser became our Defense.
Because He shared our infirmity,
He intercedes now with sympathy.

Faithful and merciful, our High Priest
Succors His children from greatest to least.
His off'ring perfected us once for all,
Sanctified and restored us from the Fall.

He died to validate His last will
But lives to administer blessings still
To those who trust Him and name His name—
Yesterday, now, and forever the same.

Slow-hearted fools were we, as He said,
But now we understand what He did.
Now we must serve him with all our might,
For He alone gives salvation and light.

— Rebecca May Hope
Ballad primarily in dactylic trimeter, aabb

Exceeding Riches

In the Beloved
I am accepted.
I am accounted
Righteous as He.
God turned the tables
When Christ resurrected:
He became sin
That I might be free.

I have an earnest—
The seal of the Spirit—
On an inheritance,
A gift from my Lord.
I am His workmanship
Warring with wickedness.
He is my armor,
His Spirit, my sword.

Even now I am seated
Above in the heavenlies,
Already a citizen
Of that glad shore.
Christ became orphaned
That I'd be adopted,
Joint-heirs with Jesus
For evermore.

— Rebecca May Hope
Ballad using primarily dactyls.

A Psalm of Thanksgiving for Faith

O Lord, our strength in tempests found,
In Your embrace, we are unbound.
Though storms may rage and skies may weep,
Our faith in You, it does not sleep.

"For therein is the righteousness of God revealed from faith to faith,"
As it is written, "The just shall live by faith."
For every trial, every test,
You've given us the strength to rest.

We thank You for the faith so strong,
That holds us fast when all is wrong.
It's in Your love, we find our peace,
And in Your grace, our fears release.

So let us sing with hearts so bold,
Of faith that never grows old.
For in Your hands, our lives are cast,
And in Your love, we're held steadfast.

— C.R. Powell
Ballad

Prayer

Prayer the church's banquet, angel's age,
God's breath in man returning to his birth,
The soul in paraphrase, heart in pilgrimage,
The Christian plummet sounding heav'n and earth

from *Prayer 1*
George Herbert, 1593—1633

Prayer Time

Prayer time
Stand before God
Letting go of the grudge
Mercy does not punish or judge
Free Grace

— Jaqueline Anderson
Cinquain

Answered Prayers

Baby was born ill
Parents prayed for her with faith
Today she's thriving

— Vanessa Caraveo
Haiku

Prayer

Prayer is the siphon dipped into a well,
the water suctioned up to revive the flowers,
a bridge hanging over grief, a sleeping pill
and the sleepless night's aching tooth, the sour
taste of told lies, a pin-light in a mine,
the unrepentant's agony of self-pity
in a waste of shame, a torch of knotty pine
dazzling the eyes, a lock that's hard to jimmy,
fasting's brother, sister of broken heart
beyond healing, an inarticulate groan
of sorrow, earth and heaven achieving two-part
harmony, the lost child's weeping for home,
a rope ladder dangling for the wary sinner,
a garden that flowers only when you enter.

— J.S. Absher
Sonnet

Publication credit: Amethyst Review, Feb. 2023

Bad Prayer

I thirst for you, I drew apart
To settle by a peaceful happy hearth
Vowing for silent solemn rectitude
To worship and love in solitude

I settled in the quiet chair
And turned my will and heart
To holy prayer

All thoughts to you! O Lovely Divine!
I give you my soul, my will
To make them thine!

When on the sill a bird appears!
He cocks his saucy head
He chirps a string of babbling nonsense
      And peers
At me as if to say
      See my lovely feathers!
      Hear my charming song!
      Now come along!
What could be more important today?

I followed him into a wood
Entranced by his warbles I followed on
Through hills, by streams, I was drawn
Until at last, his song did still
And I remembered I'd lost my will
I'd lost my way
      I had completely forgotten to pray

— Annette Moore
Mixed ballad and tercets

An Evening Prayer

Here I am again, Lord,
returning at the end of day,
repenting for repeating
what tends to be my way—

quiet when talking is needed
thinking my words have little value
when maybe there is someone
feeling encouragement pass through.

I know when I recount
kindnesses toward me
they're like water for a thirst—
like the desert needs the sea.

I ask that you restore, dear Lord,
faith again re-fired
burning anew, trusting in you
this weary soul retired—

not from the calling to find in you
renewed purpose for me here,
but retired from my internal battles
feeling alone when no one's near.

Keep me walking a little longer, Lord
with you for a day or after,
to know again the strength you give
through others' love and laughter.

— deb y. felio
Lyric poem in quatrains

I Didn't Pray

Once again, I wasted a day
Hours went by when I should have prayed
Instead, my thoughts strayed

Once again, I wasted a night
In thoughts of myself, not others' plight
I think I can't help them, but my prayers might

God forgive me those wasted hours
Help me remember prayer's power
Chide me gently, night and day
Not to waste that time away

— Annette Moore
Tercets and a quatrain

Daily Life

A whisper in the busy day
A moment where you pause to say
A simple plea or thanks above
A daily heartbeat for your love

At St. Patrick's New York City

The storied marbled floor reflects
The pilgrim face, the girl who bows
Her head entering, those whose necks

And knees are bent with newer vows.
The stained-glass gallery above,
Bejeweled with haloed, tortured brows,

Kindles in space a holy love
Or fear of God, or maybe both—
Descending, a traditional dove,

Upon a congregation loath
To concentration: one that walks
About without much aim, betrothed

To some next destination, talks
Of missed appointments here or there.
Below their feet, the marble marks

A three-word Latin questionnaire:
We all are going, but to where

— C.M. Gigliotti
Villanelle Minus

Goosebumps

faith is those goosebumps
that moment the Holy Spirit
is just there

— Jennifer Gurney
Haiku

free floating

free floating
in believing and trusting
faith

— Jennifer Gurney
Haiku

Cathedral

in a cathedral
halfway round the world
running into God

— Jennifer Gurney
Haiku

Dreams

Our dreams are precious flowers.
Ah, each one borne upon the wind
Comes-to-while-away the hours
Each blossom is a gift disinclined
To unlock her chamber -embowers.

And nourishment is required.
So we must persevere in our faith
In whatever shells get misfired
We must overcome every malaise
And somehow remain awe-inspired.

— Mark Heathcote
Rhyming cinquain

How Can I Ask

How can I ask you to speak
When my mind can never be still
But is always a clamor of thought
Wild with excitement and shrill?

— J.A. Sellers
Quatrain

Rushed Prayer

How I rush through my morning prayer
What is supposed to be my loving greeting to You
It's hard to believe it matters when I can't see you there
But Lord, oh Lord, I can certainly see
The mountains of chores I have to do

— Roberta Sachs
Loose Cinquain

Trust in Hard Times

Life meets faith in dirty trenches
Of diapers, divorce and untimely death
We send our plea and hope God quenches
The pain life brings, in every breath

The Horse and His Rider Hath He Thrown into the Sea

A man who will drown at Guadalcanal
puts five on Ocean Blue to win. His fiancée
caresses his face, calls him baby boy.
She's made her lips flamboyantly red
like the valentine the cut of the skirt
hints at between her legs. She considers
Curious Coin, almost bets on Our Boots,
but goes with the favorite, Whirlaway.
The field beats Whirlaway out of the gate. At the first
turn, trailing five lengths, jockey Arcaro sits
still as a bluepoint on the half shell. The woman
slips her hand into the pocket of her man's jacket,
shivers with excitement when in the backstretch
Arcaro takes Whirlaway to the outside and clucks.
The man, gazing through binoculars, stiffens,
and the crowd exhales a deep bass whuumph.
Wipe the jam off my mouth, says Eddie, dismounting,
with a victor's nonchalance. I been on a picnic.
When you move on him, it's like a Cadillac.

Startled by FAITH

When their child's adrift in her flesh-and-bone-
locked sea, the woman will dream of her
and the sailor, tropical currents moving
and flowing together. Then he slips from her
again, slips into the murk. She misses his hand,
his head, cannot hold the hair. In her dream
it's a dark sun's rays, it's the hair of Jesus,
the Jesus who says to her in prayer,
*Put your weight down in your heels
and clasp my mane. Relax your shoulders. Breathe.
Loosen the reins for the long race.*

— J.S. Absher
Loose iambics, with varying feet per line

Publication credit: Pinesong, 2023

Note: Italicized text in the 2nd stanza is from the account of the race by sportswriter Red Smith.

From The Path

The thorn-choked path turned many away
Thickets scratched and tore
Far easier to travel the road of ease
By bright and sunny day

But at day's end, where does each path lead?
Through the thickets, a treasure lies
The price a temporary loss, grief and pain,
The end: a soul that never dies

— Annette Moore
Quatrains

New Beginnings

Hurricane destroyed
Lost my home, left with nothing
Start anew with faith

— Vanessa Caraveo
Haiku

JOLTED

Jolted
Shocked and shaken
Cruel attack rends my heart
Healing Faith revives, I will rise
Stronger

— Jaqueline Anderson
Cinquain

Faith's a raft on a voyage

Faith's a raft on an ocean so, cling fast
it won't sink. But might you drift insane?
Might you forget even your name?
Might you drown, might you lambaste.

Might you thirst; cry deep in hunger
might you lose sight of your adventure?
Quite not all alone is the Lord's answer
Faith is a raft where you'll flounder.

So, cling fast like a stubborn barnacle,
mindful of His quietest becalm counsel
be assured: He's there keeping a vigil.

— Mark Heathcote
Quatrains and tercet

Sestina for the Lord

Alas, when nothing ever goes my way
I try to keep my goals within my sight.
I hope that they can lead to joy someday
And overpass this metaphoric night.
Among those crazy things leading to doom,
I am quite melancholic in the gloom.

My life may be infected with the gloom,
When darkness spreads its wicked wings on the way.
In waiting for the approach of the doom,
I am the girl in search of nature's sight.
When jagged rocks pinch and stick me overnight,
I search for something to lift me someday.

My faith grows stronger, and I hope someday
That winds of change will enlighten the gloom.
Faith, love, and truth will be like stars at night.
Life will be as bright as the Milky Way.
As long as righteousness is brought to light,
And lying is a sticky bomb of doom.

Startled by FAITH

I utter an impending sense of doom
Like poison killing everything someday
Or wet flowers shaking at the wind's sight.
We end with hope, and we begin in gloom,
While we're changing our lives along the way.
We're making sense of all from day to night.

As fears are left unspoken in the night,
We feel this ending is our latest doom.
Sad minds still try to find a living way.
I hope that they will save themselves someday.
They make critical changes in the gloom.
Religious leaders teach Christian sight,

When wisdom is the synonym of sight,
Blind guides are free to lead the blinds at night.
Some begin with the hope and end in gloom,
Between those sinful acts leading to doom,
They pray to God to save their souls someday.
Against all odds, they try to find their way.

At Siloam, the blind received his sight.
In working faith, the blind could leave his night
God breaks the chains; we need to leave the gloom.

— Marieta Maglas
Sestina

Gratitude

May you live in interesting times, they say
But still in trial, there's gratitude
Though times are dark and we can't see the way
May you live in interesting times, they say
Yet let us fall to our knees and pray
And see the graces with certitude
May you live in interesting times, they say
And still in trial, there's gratitude

— Roberta Sachs
Triolet

To Walk in Faith

My Lord, You give visions and dreams
But only a glimpse beyond the veil
My lord, you don't mind my struggle, it seems
Do You really trust me to prevail?

You call me to walk in shadowed way
I beg you to give me the smallest light
To see where you're leading me day by day
Yet You insist I walk by faith, not sight

So if on blind faith, oh Lord, You insist
To go the breadth, the width, the length
To trust in this darkness, and to persist
Then grant me the will and grant me the strength

— J.A. Sellers
Quatrains

Faith and Doubt

Life meets faith in dirty trenches
Of diapers, divorce and untimely death
We send our plea and hope God quenches
The pain life brings, with every breath

Awe, Atonement, and Adulation

When the Days of Awe came 'round
The Day of Atonement loomed heavy
I'd brace myself for fasting
Emptied my pockets of crumbs into the sea

The Day of Atonement loomed heavy
I paraded before me my sins
Emptied my pockets of crumbs into the sea
Breadcrumbs floated away carrying wrongs

I paraded before me my sins
Perhaps the Almighty would forgive me
Breadcrumbs floated away carrying wrongs
I promised atonement on an empty stomach

Perhaps the Almighty would forgive me
Inscribe me in the Book of Life
I promised atonement on an empty stomach
No water passed my parched lips

Inscribe me in the Book of Life
I begged and pleaded all day in shul
No water passed my parched lips
If not this Book, keep secret how I pass

I begged and pleaded all day in shul
Resentment planted a seed in me
If not this Book, keep secret how I pass
I envied those with unyielding faith

Resentment planted a seed in me
Why does the Almighty need adulation?
I envied those with unyielding faith
Search my conscience before you judge

Why does the Almighty need adulation?
I no longer brace myself for fasting
Search my conscience before you judge
When the Days of Awe come 'round

— Evie Groch
Pantoum

A Voice Calls Out In Quiet Soul

A voice calls out in quiet words
A voice calls out in quiet soul
Whispers a thundering melody
That heals and makes me whole

A voice calls out in quiet soul
A voice so soft yet strong
In this loud and tainted world
It's the voice for which I long

The voice calls out again and again
Yet I question and I doubt
The voice speaks gently day by day
What's it all about?

An unrestrained imagination
Or merely wishful thinking
False hope I grasp in deep despair
The days I feel I'm sinking?

Voice, call out in quiet words
Voice call out to quiet soul
Whisper Your thundering melody
Whisper Your words that make me whole

— J.A. Sellers
Quatrains

Faith

used Christmas wraps
my origami boat
sailing toward God

tree ornaments
clattering in the wind
my wavering faith

alone on Christmas
Jesus and I
clink our teacups

singing His praises
my off tunes corrected
by the Lord

— Jackie Chou
Haiku

Complaint

I struggle to believe that my prayers reach your ears
All alone in this valley of tears
Walking alone between shadows and fears

My God, have You forsaken me?
Turned your back and set me free
Of the love and care You promised me?

What have I done to anger You?
What microscope have You looked through?
My sins are great, and yet so few
Compared to those whom You give blessings to

— Annette Moore
Tercets and a quatrain of rhymed couplets

Prayer for Another

I lift my face to You
A face long stained with tears
Beseeching as I so long have
But nothing's changed in all these years

My heart cries out for one I love,
For him I loved so dear
When I pray for another instead of myself
Will you finally hear?

— J.A. Sellers
Quatrains

Redemption

We make mistakes and fail
He meets us in our place
Whether weak or frail
And lifts us to His Face

Second Chance

It is too late now in my life to bloom
no more will I believe
there is still time
when years have passed
when paths have been abandoned
my hope of what could be
laid aside for others
these seeds from pomegranate
broken open, spilled out beauty
what container can hold it all
how they sparkle and bite
I wanted more from my dreams
so easily traded in
believing others' happiness could be mine
I know now wind beneath wings is not flying

— deb y. felio
Reverse poem

The Path

The path
Steep twisting turns
Night closing in, off course
Prayer illuminates my way back
To You

— Jaqueline Anderson
Cinquain

Transformation

God the Transformer
In lessons of light
Gave the sick strength
And gave the blind sight.

But the greatest example
Of God's transformation
Took hatred's symbol,
Cruelty's manifestation,

The fearful Roman cross,
Man's grand work of horror—
Made from it an altar of peace
And neutralized its terror.

See! Now it stands the altar
Where peace offering was made.
There God, the Exchanger, offered His Son
As the means of spiritual trade.

The seeker brings anger,
Frustration, guilt, and pride—
And leaves them at the altar
Where the spotless Lamb has died.

By faith, he takes from the altar peace
And reconciliation.
And now a new communion
Replaces the old separation.

And as the sparrows nested in
Those amiable altars of old,
So the seeker finds his peace at last
In the arms of his risen Lord.

— Rebecca May Hope
Ballad using both dactylic and iambic lines. Every other line rhymes

Prison Hours

The Hillsville, Virginia, Courthouse Massacre, March 14, 1912
Down highway 58, from 220
into Hillsville, cars are stopping at yard sales
in front of homes, gas stations, and salons
to buy stopped clocks, cane-bottomed chairs on wheels,

burnished silver mirrors in which the buyer
admires the self rippling in the frame,
and old glass, browns and blues unstoppered,
that once gave of nostrums or perfume.

We've not come to buy. We've driven for hours
to see the old courthouse, to count each hole
the bullets gouged in the stairway and the courtroom,
to guess where the shooters stood, the dead fell:

the judge and sheriff; a juror; the prosecutor
who'd come to court, unused to guns but armed;
a witness gut shot and throwing up,
angrily insisting she was not harmed.

Someone fired first: some Allen, the crowd
decided (the loudest in the crowd decides)—
Floyd on the stand or Sidna from his seat.
True, both were armed and ready to fight,

but so were they all. Floyd was wounded, captured
with his son, and tried. Sidna went on the run,
lived by adze and saw till caught, hauled home,
imprisoned; his house seized; his family thrown

penniless on the street; the fruit trees razed.
He might have lived on fantasies of revenge
but woodwork and the Good Book made
him scrounge for wood; work it into edge
and angle with knife and prayer, sorrow and plane;
his first two years apprenticed to rage and shame.

****

Nights, he dreamed his wife drew long black hair
taut and fingered a country waltz; his older
girl, all in blue, sang, Papa, I'll be true;
the younger in red wept singing into his shoulder
Papa, I'd rather be dead. He made the most
beautiful things he could imagine as solace
for their sorrow, from items found or smuggled
into prison, from fragments of the life they'd lost—
parasol handle, imported; hair-brush, cherry;
window-sash, butter box, maul, and curry comb—
carved and fitted, dark wood next to light
pad-cut or beveled, an intricate herringbone

of mental calculation and hands' cunning,
conspiring, days on end, to keep his slow time running.

****

He emptied hours by filling them—thirty-five
hundred to make his first table, eleven
years to finish the twenty pieces he lived on
in old age: three more tables; ten
treasure boxes, empty; four cups, ditto;
a suitcase (he dreamed of seeing the Holy Land);
a vase. Thirty-five hundred hours to imagine
revenge, then let it go. He was pardoned
when justice at last acknowledged no one knew
who fired first, or who killed whom (too late
for Floyd and son, both sent to the chair).
Though that day he had gone to court, hate
in the heart, a gun in the pocket, and fired,
and thereby he owed his life, or not much less,
he had still greater debts—his daughters' ruined
childhoods, his wife's lost happiness.
I know this guilt—engine and obstacle;
a bed to lie in; a rash; a vehicle.

****

Startled by FAITH

In his last years, when notoriety
drew crowds to his marquetry, 8th wonder
of the world!, for a few bits a head, the folks
meeting the soft-spoken man would blunder
by showing the disappointment of the monsters
they'd bottled up that hoped to meet a monster.
"Are you really the Mister Sidna Allen?"
they asked. He was, perhaps, no longer,
but it was the name he answered to, the one
engraved on his stone, maybe on heaven's roll.
At his last, best showing, thousands saw him buried.
He'd planed and shimmed himself into a role
of honor—light wood next to dark, a fiddly
moral puzzle. The veneer pieced crosswise
over old Adam from scraps of family love,
heavenly hopes, and broken lives

held; blood no longer called for blood
He was his handiwork and it was good.

— Stan Absher
Ballad stanzas, with each section ending in a rhymed couplet.

Powerless Alone

When we cry and call for self-reliance,
We find a set of pulleys and a hoist.
We acquiesce and suffer our defiance,
And give it sway, and reckon it by voice -
We open up an ear to hear the silence,
In doubt that we'll find reason to rejoice.
At any point. We stand a slave to science:
The chemistry prevails above the noise.

Without acknowledgment that our defect
Will stare - imperious - fail to feel our pain,
So that we homage pay in all effect,
The cycle is perpetually insane:
The harm we most despise we do select,
Denying while we start the silent train,
The failure to preside, thus we reject
The efficacy we had hoped to gain

Step one toward victory is oddly lame
In that the bottom signals our defeat.
Unless we take the loss to start the game,
We cannot foment progress in retreat.
Alone, then, everything must stay the same,
But by relinquishing the driver's seat,
We give ourselves a chance to lay a claim
To blaze a future trail on hopeful streets.

— Phil Repko
Ballad

Full Disclosure

Between the wall and you and me
We'll keep communication free,
And peel back layers - secret scarred -
In camouflage, secured by bars.
I'm told I have no forward way
Without an honest repartee`
With one who vows to watch my back
And intercept the next attack
I privately intend to wage
Against myself. Still fueled by rage
That likewise cowers underground
And rarely overtakes a sound

Like confidence or self-respect.
I lack the nerve to self-reflect.
Thus no one knew for many years,
The public grin hid private tears.
So now I undertake the risk
To here divulge by hit and miss
The range and scope of lethal sins
Within a game that no one wins,
To which I have been so long chained.
Sincerity feels cold and strange.
I cross my heart and pray for luck
That three of us maintain the pluck
To honor right this deal we've struck:
Myself, the sponsor, Him above.

— Phil Repko
Ballad

Taking Stock

It's not as if I haven't known the whole ride down the hill,
The sources of my ballast - all the weight that helped me tilt
The perch in the direction that might mitigate the flaws,
Regardless if they qualify as tragic. Still I call
On what is left of honor or of courage on this trek
To salvage what is left of what I'll call my self-respect.
For one, I've summoned up great patience in my worst duress,
But then fell short of even decent empathy when tests
Deplete my sense of progress toward a higher goal. I guess
I'm guilty too of callousness and snide dismissiveness.
I can be loathe to listen, slow to proffer true respect.

Awareness by itself is not enough. When I reflect
Upon the times I've sold far short both friend and wary foe,
I take responsibility for falling shorter. Though
The road will not be silky smooth, and I will surely fret.
If you will walk with me, I feel, I will recover yet.
To put the liabilities in full view plants a seed,
That may grow tall and strong with proper care. This is my creed:
That I will make commitment to foresee my better self,
And making strides to be as much, I'll will myself to health.

— Phil Repko
Ballad

The Cross One Bears

      Quite early came the contradictory call
      To be at once a cynic and yet cursed
      With idealistic certainty that all
      May yet be done correctly, though the worst

      Is surely lurking somewhere in the space
      Between the well-intentioned and the good,
      The push and pull, the yin and yang - the race
      Conducted just as if he'd understood

      That no one ever really makes the grade.
      He knows that he's not getting out alive,
      And thus he bears the brunt. The price is paid
      When disappointment casts a constant slide.

      The cross he bears is knowledge that he dies
      With every forward step, and yet he lacks
      Autonomy to deviate. He tries
      To lie to his own self; obscure his tracks.

A contradiction this: the only choice
We really get is putting on the face
That might beguile the time and curb the voice
Which wants to scream, but abdicates - with grace.

— *Phil Repko*
Quatrains

From the Bible

Isaiah 53 Sonnetized

A root, a tender plant from arid ground
Has sprung up, giving life to lifeless man.
Despised, rejected, formless, He was found
A man of sorrows. Yet His work began:
For our transgressions was He sorely bruised;
To gain our peace was Christ, the Servant, killed;
For our iniquities He was abused,
And with His bloody stripes, mankind is healed.
Though just, before His shearers He was dumb
And opened not His mouth. It satisfied—
Yes, pleased—the Lord to bruise Him, so that some
Through knowledge of Him might be justified.
  He bore the sins of many so that we
  Can stand before him purified and free.

— Rebecca May Hope
Shakespearean (English) sonnet

Poet's note on this set of poems: They are written in iambic pentameter and follow the rhyme scheme *ababcdcdefefgg*. I wrote these as a way to practice the sonnet form and meditate on the scripture passages at the same time. Writing these helped me improve as a poet and enhanced my understanding of the passages and my faith.

James 3 Sonnetized

The one who owns an inoffensive tongue
Can claim a perfect score before the Lord.
That little member boasts in old and young,
Defiles them with each evil, fiery word.
For ev'ry kind of beast is tamed by men,
But our own tongue remains forever wild.
That noxious and unstable charlatan
Has cursed, then blessed, then flattered, then reviled.
Whoever seeks the key to being wise
Must banish from his ways all bitter strife.
For godly wisdom's kind, wears no disguise,
Is pure, accessible, and brings forth life.
   Let those who sow in righteousness ne'er cease
   Their quiet labor for a life of peace.

— Rebecca May Hope
Shakespearean (English) sonnet

The Way

In this land where predators feed upon prey
And the trusting are maimed and devoured
Time after time and day after day
One longs for kindness to become empowered.

As men and women seem destined for strife
And children suffer due to their struggle
Being human is a stumbling block for life
That keeps families from getting to cuddle.

In school and work, brutal bullies form cliques
Relishing hindering those of character
Through their machinations and politics
Silencing the voice of good choristers.

The immoral seize all opportunity
While the disciplined are left to plod on
As the cheaters enjoy immunity
From the wrongs that they continually spawn.

The rich plunder and plague upon the poor
Then turn around and fault them for their fate
Thereby rationalizing their hauteur
While their poverty they worked to create.

In contrast, Jesus the poor did not plunder
But walked in their midst and blessed the humble
The money changers' tables he tore asunder
Knowing they caused the needy to stumble.

Respecting women and their testimony
He entrusted them to spread The Good News
That Christ was risen in perfect harmony
Just as he said, the world with light to infuse.

That children can enter The Kingdom of Heaven
And are not to be harmed, but protected
Was a novel truth in making them even
As all who believe in Him are respected.

Unimpressed by guile, Christ blesses the pure in heart
Welcoming to Him, those who do what is right

For by their fruits their virtue stands apart
Regardless of their status or social plight.

Giving us The Door that opens up for good
In Jesus, the kind are not prey, but to pray
God's power for good to unleash as we should
As Jesus is The Truth, and The Life, and The Way.

— Luisa Reyes
Ballad

Psalm 19 Sonnetized

The heavens shout with praises to the Lord
And echo back His knowledge and his grace
With poetry that cannot be ignored,
With imagery that nothing can erase.
The perfect law of God converts the soul;
His testimonies make the simple wise;
His statutes cause rejoicing chants to roll;
And each commandment luminates the eyes.
They ought to be desired more than gold,
For keeping them ensures a great reward.
Please cleanse me from the secret sins I hold
And keep me innocent before you, Lord.
      May every meditation of my heart
      Please You as morning dawns and duties start.

— Rebecca May Hope
Shakespearean (English) sonnet

Wings of Demon, *Wings of Dove*

Wings of demon, wings of dove
Marbled black and satin gray
Both may fly and both may fall
But only one was promised all

Promised pleasure, promised praise
Promised dominion over his days
The Dove was promised heartache and pain
Nights in cold and rain-drenched trees

Both may fly and both may fall
But only one will conquer all
Wings of demon, wings of dove
Delivered from dark, delivered by love

— Angela Rose
Quatrains

The Women of Jerusalem

Falling down on trembling knee
Full of pain to see His bloodied face
I wept for Christ of Galilee

I met Him the day He heeded my plea
and healed my Son at the watering place
Falling down on trembling knee

It breaks my heart to see such ignominy
Heaped on this gentle Man of Grace
I wept for Christ of Galilee

"Weep for yourselves," he said, "Not me.
For terror is coming to the human race.
Falling down on trembling knee

Saying, the barren one, blest is she
For no child of hers will suffer this disgrace."
I wept for Christ of Galilee

Then He stumbled on, the rabble shouting in glee
As He went to Golgotha to set us free
Falling down on trembling knee
I wept for Christ of Galilee

— Christina Lincoln
Villanelle

Christina's poems in this book are from her work in progress, The Passion Cycle, *a historically researched re-telling of the events and people of Christ's passion, in poetry.*

Simon of Cyrene

There in the city, we'd journeyed to reach
Over nine hundred miles, all the way from Cyrene,
to faithfully keep the paschal feast,
In the holy city we'd never before seen.

Bustled and jostled and pushed by the crowd
As a convict beneath his heavy cross fell
His eyes met mine, his bleeding back bowed
 A Centurion wrenched my arm; compelled

Me to lift the heavy beam
And carry it beside the bloodied man
Who stumbled beside me with blood that streamed
Into his eyes, on shoulder, on hand

A thousand fears washed through my head
Fears for my sons, my name, my life
As I followed where this condemned man led
Watching his back, bent over with strife.

Down the streets of the city, shackled and chained,
Through a crowd roaring with spittle and jeers,
A thousand throats calling his name
And then I heard women—pity and tears.

They wept for him yet he dried their tears
Saying, I am not the one to mourn
But cry for women in future years
Who have not nursed, nor children borne

I turned my head; his eyes met mine
What man was this who hardly cared
For pain of scourging, back and spine,
But wept for how another fared?

My vision changed, I hefted the wood
Shameful ignominy seemed now gain
I carried it, praying, for a man who was good
I wanted only to ease his pain

I bore His cross to the place of the Skull
Where the Man was nailed onto the wood
His eyes eternal, deep, and full
Bearing His cross was my greatest good

— Christina Lincoln
Rhyming quatrains

GESTES

Romans
Must leave our land
For that I'll gladly die
Holy Man indeed! He fails us!
Deep hate!

Jesu
Called Yourself God
So save Yourself and us!
Come down off that cross if You're God!
Fraud! Fake!

— Christina Lincoln
Two cinquains

Tradition names the Good and Bad Thieves, who hung on crosses on either side of Jesus, as Dismas and Gestes respectively.

DISMAS

Guilty
I have done wrong
I will die for my sins
Beside this holy man renowned
Blessing

Raised high for my sins
Beside Him who will be raised
For eternity
Remember me...when You come
Into Your kingdom oh Lord

— Christina Lincoln
Two cinquains

Mother & Son

John, see your Mother
To be with you here on earth
Mother, see your son
Watch over my beloved
And my Chosen for all time

— Christina Lincoln
Tatanka

Father, Forgive Them

Father, forgive them
For they know not what they do
Father forgive them
They know not the Son of Man
When they see Him on this Cross

— Christina Lincoln
Tatanka

centurion

he offered him gall	on a sponge	on a spear
while he hung	on a cross	made of wood
on a mound	at a place	of the skull
Golgotha	where a man	trained to kill
by the cross	on a hill	saw the sky
turning grey	in those eyes	cast to heaven
love for him	love for all	in this world
and the man	on the cross	who had suffered
who had dared	to show love	even now
as he dared	to die here	to save him
who heard	distant thunder	rattling breath
at long last	he hefted	the spear
aimed it well	jabbed	in his side
this dying man	this god	that gushed water
and then water	burst forth	from the sky
turned to gray	turned to green	turned to black

— Donna Isaac
Contrapuntal poem

Death & the Afterlife

What waits for us beyond this earthly door?
What waits for us beyond our earthly days
Do you believe you'll live forevermore?
Then choose wisely in all your ways.

Newly Buried Grandmother Prepares to Enter the Pearly Gates

Heavier than she can ever
remember, the rain is falling in spades.
On her roof enormous hands
      pound boom-lay, boom-lay.

This is her mother's belly, an oven
stoked with wet kindling, a sway
in the rockabye of a tree. She rests
      where ramblers wait.

Dressed in a gold neck scarf they've pinned
with a silver brooch to match her hair,
lonely carp where river deepens
into hole and lair,
she ponders scaled and plated creatures
that spawn and perish in silt
and clay; and waxy chalcedony
and massive flint
that could strike or catch
fire in the air, but work in the mud
a hidden purpose: she weighs the forms
of widowhood.
Those who arm-in-arm have mourned,
she sees them home, couple and uncouple,

Startled by FAITH

sees each fall to a separate dream
and reach for a secret double—
a body miraculously winged and hoofed,
built for the long race and the short dash,
to give without tiring, to take without theft,
thewed like the blacksnake and ash.
She sees God angling for us all,
hooking and crooking those well-worn lines.
She is lured by the dark, impermeable gleam
of that many-fractured mind.

— J.S. Absher
Rhymes abab

Publication credit: Inscape, Winter 2024.
Originally published in J.S. Absher, The Burial of Anyce Shepherd, Main Street Rag Publications, 2006.

Imminent just before death

Your voice is like fruit under-ripened
Your hair needs to turn a silvery grey,
Your thoughts need to weep like a cloud
And pave the ground in a creeping moss
Your fingers need to wither like coffin nails
And palms roll out a ball of unravelling-yarn
But your eyes need to glint like white jasmine
And strike and put the moonlight in fear
And then and only then, will they learn
About your wisdom, your solemn truth
About your knowledge and faith
And listen to what you have in abundance to say.

— Mark Heathcote
Ode

On the Death of the Monarch
9 September 2022

If it is true that one from far afield
Can hear an empire lay itself to rest
For one to whom her subjects all appealed,
Herself now subject to the final test;
That even now the day of judgment's hid
From sovereigns, rogues, and commoners alike
In spite of all their vain attempt to bid
For hints of Fate, forewarnings of its strike;
That death and birth, to finish and begin,
Continue to collide in blind regard
For neither going out nor coming in,
And that the way is narrow, short, and barred;
That those divine must also have an end
And glory with disgrace must disappear—
Then let hers be the moment I attend.
The curfew tolls the knell, and I am here.

— CM Gigliotti
Sonnet Plus

I Commend My Spirit

Since the world, I know, has not stopped spinning,
And still I feel, suspended in a way.
I felt so certain at the beginning
That near the end I'd know just what to say.

But knowledge, wisdom? Nothing trounces fear.
By small degrees the threats have taken shape,
To gain control of moments drawing near
To this, the final breath, the last escape.

In other words, thank God I've reached the line -
I know it's writ in sand - at least for me -
The fault lies in the stars when stars are mine,
But otherwise, it is humanity

That needs to see that they may follow me,
The instant they acknowledge there's no choice.
Free Will exists, without dexterity.
No need to scream if one abjures his voice.

The moral then: the end is not the end.
One brand of spinning supersedes the rest.
The boundaries fall away once we expend
The final, mortal, cleansing, deathly breath.

I've told you all along, "Be not afraid,"
The darkest force is sapping abject fear.
No one would follow onward, had I stayed.
You must not be resigned to tarry here…

— Phil Repko
Ballad

POETRY FORMS

Abecederian

The abecederian has 26 lines, the first letter of each line making the alphabet.

Ballad

A ballad typically is a story told in stanzas of four lines with the second and fourth lines rhyming.

Cinquain

5 lines, similar to haiku and tanka.

Lines 1 and 5 have 2 syllables.

Lines 2, 3, and 4 have more syllables, giving them a diamond shape.

They should tell a small story with action, feeling, and a conclusion.

Contrapuntal

Contrapuntal poetry weaves together two or more poems and can be read different ways. They should have a visual form on the page.

Haiku

3 lines of 5 syllables, 7 syllables, 5 syllables.

Lyric Poem

Lyric poetry focuses on emotions. In ancient times, a lyric poem was always accompanied by instrumental music.

Ode

Odes are typically poems of praise. It should be solemn and serious in tone. It should have uniform metrical feet but this is often not strictly observed. Traditional odes include Pindar, Horatian, and irregular.

Pantoum

A series of quatrains of ABAB, in which the second rhyme (B) becomes the first rhyme of the next quatrain. So ABAB BCBC CDCD DEDE etc.

Reverse poem

A reverse poem can be read from the top to bottom or from the bottom line to he top. Usually, the poem means the complete opposite when read in reverse.

Rondeau

A 13-line poem divided into stanzas of 5, 3, and 5 lines with only two rhymes through. The opening words of the first line become a refrain at the end of the second and third stanzas.

Sestina

A sestina has seven stanzas. The first six have six lines each, and the last, the *envoi*, has three. Each line of the first six stanzas ends with one of the same six words. The *envoi* uses three of these final words.

Sonnet

Sonnets are 14 lines, traditionally 8 lines and then 6. They typically use iambic pentameter and a rhyme scheme. There are several variations on the sonnet:

Italian, or Petrarchan: rhyme scheme of ABBA ABBA followed by either CDEDCE or CDCDCD.

English, Shakespearean, or Elizabethan: rhyme scheme AB AB CDCD EFEF GG

In a sonnet, the first 8 lines typically propose a problem or ask a question. The question is answered in the last 6 lines.

Tanka

A Japanese poem of five lines. The first and third have five syllables; the second, fourth, and fifth have seven syllables. It should give a complete picture of an event or mood.

Triolet

The triolet has 8 lines, usually of 8 syllables each. Rhyme scheme ABaAabAB. Thus, the first, fourth, and seventh lines are identical. The second and eighth lines are identical. The third, fifth, and sixth lines rhyme with either A or B.

Villanelle

19 lines; five tercets (three-line stanzas) of ABA with a quatrain (four lines) at the end with ABAA. The first and third lines of the first tercet alternate as the final lines of the following tercets and form the last two lines of the last quatrain.

POET BIOS

FEATURED POET

J.S. Absher

J.S. Absher has published two full-length books of poetry, *Skating Rough Ground* (Kelsay Press, 2022) and *Mouth Work* (St. Andrews University Press), winner of the 2015 Lena Shull Award from the North Carolina Poetry Society. His poems have won awards from *BYU Studies Quarterly, Dialogue: A Journal of Mormon Thought,* and the *North Carolina Poetry Society, and* they have been nominated several times for the Pushcart Prize and the Best of the Net.

His work has been published by *Triggerfish Critical Review, Tar River Poetry, The McNeese Review, New Verse Review,* and more. He is seeking to publish his memoir of his father, *Slipping: Rise and Fall of a Country Banker*. His next book is a group portrait of fifty men who in 1895 put their lives on the line to prevent a rumored lynching. Results of his research are posted on his website for comment.

Absher lives in Raleigh, NC, with his wife, Patti.

www.jsabsherpoetry.com
Www.jsabsherpoetry.com/pluck-enough.html#/

ALL POETS

Jaqueline Anderson

Jackie lives on the Texas gulf coast. Her work has been published in many anthologies. She enjoys traveling with her husband, visiting with her grandchildren & cooking vegan foods. She loves short form poetry and hopes to publish her own collection of poems in the near future.

Vanessa Caraveo

Vanessa Caraveo is an award-winning bilingual author, published poet, and artist who has a passion for promoting inclusion, empowerment and equality for all, helping others discover the power they possess within themselves to overcome adversity and persevere in life. Her work brings focus to many social issues that exist in today's world and has been published in *Literature Today Journal*, *Poetrybay*, *The Raven Review*, *Anacua Literary Arts Journal*, and in various anthologies throughout the years.

Jackie Chou

Jackie Chou is a writer from Southern California who has two collections of poetry, *The Sorceress* and *Finding My Heart in Love and Loss*, published by cyberwit. Her poem "Formosa" was a finalist in the Stephen A DiBiase Poetry Prize. She has work forthcoming in Synchronised Chaos in August 2024.

Deb Y. Felio

deb y felio, in Boulder Colorado, writes late at night on the mundane and the miraculous in all of life. Her work is published online and in print, including anthologies: Hay(na)ku 15; Minnie's Diary, A Southern Literary Review October (2018); and Gabriel's Horn: Startled by Joy and Startled by Nature (2020), Refuse to Stay Silent (2020) commemorating the centennial of the 19th amendment, I-70 Review, 2022. Her acrostic was published in How to Write a Form Poem by Tania Runyan, and her untitled cherita sequence was a finalist in the MacQueens's Quarterly March 2021 ekphrastic challenge.

C.M. Gigliotti

C.M. Gigliotti is a multi-hyphenate artist with degrees from Central Connecticut State University and the Writers Institute at Susquehanna University. Her poetry appears in *CommuterLit, The Twin Bill, Rough Cut Press, MEMEZINE, Songs of Eretz, Prose Poems,* and elsewhere. She also writes on Substack at *Così faccio io*. She has lived in Germany since 2019.

Evie Groch

Evie Groch's opinion pieces, humor, poems, short stories, and recipes have been published in the New York Times, The SF Chronicle, The Contra Costa Times, The Journal, Games Magazine, in various anthologies and online. Her themes are travel, languages, immigration and justice of which she writes in *Half the Hurricanes*.

Jennifer Gurney

Jennifer Gurney lives in Colorado where she teaches, paints, writes and hikes. Her poetry has appeared internationally in a wide variety of journals, two of her poems have won international contests and one was recently turned into a choral piece for a concert. Jennifer's first book of poetry, *My Eyes Adjusting,* has recently been published.

Jerri Hardesty

Jerri Hardesty lives in the woods of Alabama with husband, Kirk, also a writer. They run the nonprofit poetry organization, New Dawn Unlimited, Inc. (NewDawnUnlimited.com). Jerri has had over 700 poems published and has won more than 2400 awards and titles in both written and spoken word/performance poetry.

Mark Heathcote

Mark Andrew Heathcote is an adult learning difficulties support worker. He has poems published in journals, magazines, and anthologies online and in print. He resides in the UK and is from Manchester. Mark is the author of "In Perpetuity" and "Back on Earth," two books of poems published by Creative Talents Unleashed.

Rebecca May Hope

Rebecca May Hope teaches writing at a homeschool academy and a liberal arts university. Her longer works include two historical fiction novels and an award-winning contemporary Christian novella. Her short works—memoirs and short stories—have been published in anthologies and online literary magazines. She lives in Champlin, Minnesota, with her husband, who is also an author.

Christina Lincoln

Christina is a poet and writer. Her greatest love is her family—her husband, six children, and two mastiffs. With several children raised and out in the world, she now devotes more time to writing, poetry, and gardening. A native of the coast of Maine, Christina is a great lover of any and all seafood—especially with white wine.

Marieta Maglas

Marieta has been published in The MockingOwl Roost, Lothlorien Journal, Verse-Virtual, Silver Birch Press, Sybaritic Press, Kingfisher Poetry, Oddville Press, Prolific Press, Dashboard Horus, Coin-Operated Press, Mayari Literature, Synchronized Chaos, Al-Khemia Poetica, PentaCat Press, and many more.

Annette Moore

Annette is a native of Virginia, currently living in New England where she loves to garden and visit the ocean, both of which are favorite subjects of her writing. After many years in business, she began writing in 2016. She loves poetry for its ability to speak great truths and wisdom succinctly and in unique ways.

C.R. Powell

Dr. Powell is an author, poet, musician, engineering and management consultant and aspiring polymath with his fingers on everything from fretboards and ivories to the pulse of post-modernism, surrealism, and nihilism's impact on morality and sanity. His work takes him from supercomputers to AI. In his spare time, he's an inventor.

Phil Repko

Phil Repko has been a teacher, coach, and school administrator for 42 years, but he has been writing in multiple genres for even longer. He is celebrating the publication of his first book, *Pieces of April*, a collection of more than 100 poems, recently released by Anxiety Press.

Luisa Reyes

Luisa Kay Reyes' essay, "Thank You", is the winner of the April 2017 memoir contest of "The Dead Mule School Of Southern Literature". Her Christmas poem was a first place winner in the 16th Annual Stark County District Library Poetry Contest. Additionally, her essay "My Border Crossing" received a Pushcart Prize nomination from the Port Yonder Press. And two of her essays have been nominated for the "Best of the Net" anthology. With one of her essays recently being featured on "The Dirty Spoon" radio hour.

Angela Rose

Angela is pleased to be publishing her first poetry. She attends college in the Midwest, studying biology and active in her church.

Roberta Sachs

In the hours after her day job as a veterinarian, Roberta likes to relax with a glass of red wine and a book of poetry. While a fan of Keats and Yeats, or Kates and Yates as she likes to call them, she finds herself drawn to writing more humorous observations drawn from her love of animals and the natural world. She can on occasion write more serious observations.

J.A. Sellers

After growing up on a farm in Nebraska, J.A. Sellers earned degrees in philosophy and English, which led, through unexpected twists and turns, to a career in finance and banking, which led to the opportunity to travel, particularly to Eastern Europe and Asia, to study many cultures, and return finally to writing and poetry. J.A. Sellers is currently working on a first book of poetry.

Tekkan

Barry MacDonald goes by the *dharma* name "*Tekkan*," which means "Iron Man" in 13th century Japanese. *Tekkan* indicates a "settled practitioner of great determination." He was given this name when he took Buddhist vows.

Tekkan was the featured poet in the 2022 volume of *Startled by Laughter* and was in the top ten of 2,000 poets published by the first issue of *Maplestaple* in a literary contest in 2023. He has also been published in numerous publications.

Editor

Laura Vosika

Laura Vosika is the author of *The Blue Bells Chronicles*, a tale of time travel, action and adventure, romance and redemption, across modern and medieval Scotland. She has had poetry published in *The Mocassin* and *Martin Lake Journal*. Her first collection of music has been released under the name *Glenmirril Garden*. She co-hosts *Books and Brews with Laura Vosika and Chris Powell*, which interviews authors and poets while pairing their work to beer or cocktails. Laura has been featured in newspapers and on radio and TV, in addition to being on numerous podcasts and blogs.

She is the mother of ten, currently living in the Appalachians with her husband, their Irish Wolfhound Liadan, Bernese Mountain Dog Boo Bear, and their rabbits, sheep, and chickens on Glenmirril Farm.

www.lauravosika.com
www.glenmirrilfarms.wordpress.com
www.booksandbrews.net

AFTERWORD

We hope you have enjoyed *Startled by FAITH* and found some joy, peace, inspiration and thought-provoking ideas within these pages! If you've enjoyed the book, please help our poets gain well-deserved recognition by leaving a review, following them at their social media, or buying a copy of the book for your fellow poetry-lovers.

At Gabriel's Horn, we offer a paying market to quality poets working in traditional forms. The *Startled by* series is an annual publication. We invite you to submit to our upcoming volumes:

2025   Children
2026   America
2027   Legend and Lore
2028   War and Peace
2029   Freedom
2030   Courage

These are subject to change, particularly if we receive enough submissions to put out two anthologies per year. Our most current information is at   www.gabrielshornpress.com/poetry-anthology or contact gabrielshorpress@gmail.com

Index

Absher, J.S.
    Earthworm Lore   2
    Newly Buried Grandmother
        Prepares to Enter the Pearly Gates 100
    Prayer   33
    Prison Hours   70
    The Horse and His Rider
        He Hath Thrown into the Sea   46

Anderson, Jacqueline
    JOLTED   50
    Prayer Time   32
    The Path   67

Caraveo, Vanessa
    Answered Prayers   32
    New Beginnings   50

Chou, Jackie
    Faith   62

Felio, Deb Y.
    Abercedarian Alleluia   18
    An Evening Prayer   36
    Second Chance   66

Gigliotti, C.M.
    At St. Patrick's, New York City   40
    On the Death of a Monarch   103

Groch, Evie
    Awe, Atonement, and Adulation   58
    Villanelle in Prayer   8

Gurney, Jennifer
    Cathedral   42
    free floating   42
    Goosebumps   42

Hardesty, Jerri
    Faithful Bumblebee   16

Heathcote, Mark
    Dreams   43
    Faith's a Raft on a Voyage   51
    Imminent Just Before Death   102

Hope, Rebecca May
    After Emmaus   26
    Exceeding Riches   28
    Incarnation   22
    Isaiah 53 Sonnetized   84
    James 3 Sonnetized   85
    Psalm 19 Sonnetized   88
    Thanksgiving   24
    Transformation   68

Isaac, Donna
    Centurion   97
    Science Class   4

Lincoln, Christina
- *Dismas* — 95
- *Father, Forgive Them* — 96
- *Gestes* — 94
- *Mother & Son* — 96
- *Simon of Cyrene* — 92
- *The Women of Jerusalem* — 90

Maglas, Marieta
- *Sestina for the Lord* — 52

Moore, Annette
- *Bad Prayer* — 34
- *Complaint* — 63
- *from The Path* — 48
- *I Didn't Pray* — 38

Powell, C.R.
- *A Psalm of Thanksgiving* — 29
- *An Ode to Faith* — 20

Repko, Phil
- *Full Disclosure* — 76
- *I Commend My Spirit* — 104
- *Powerless Alone* — 74
- *Taking Stock* — 78
- *The Cross One Bears* — 80

Reyes, Luisa
- *The Way* — 86

Rose, Angela
- *The Stump* — 6
- *Wings of Demon, Wings of Dove* — 89

Sachs, Roberta
    Gratitude   54
    Rushed Prayer   44

Sellers, J.A.
    A Voice Calls Out in Quiet Soul   60
    How Can I Ask?   44
    Prayer for Another   64
    Stalking the Deer   10
    To Walk in Faith   55

Tekkan
    Sand   14
    Where Did Yesterday Go?   12

www.ingramcontent.com/pod-product-compliance
Lightning Source LLC
Chambersburg PA
CBHW060837050426
42453CB00008B/727